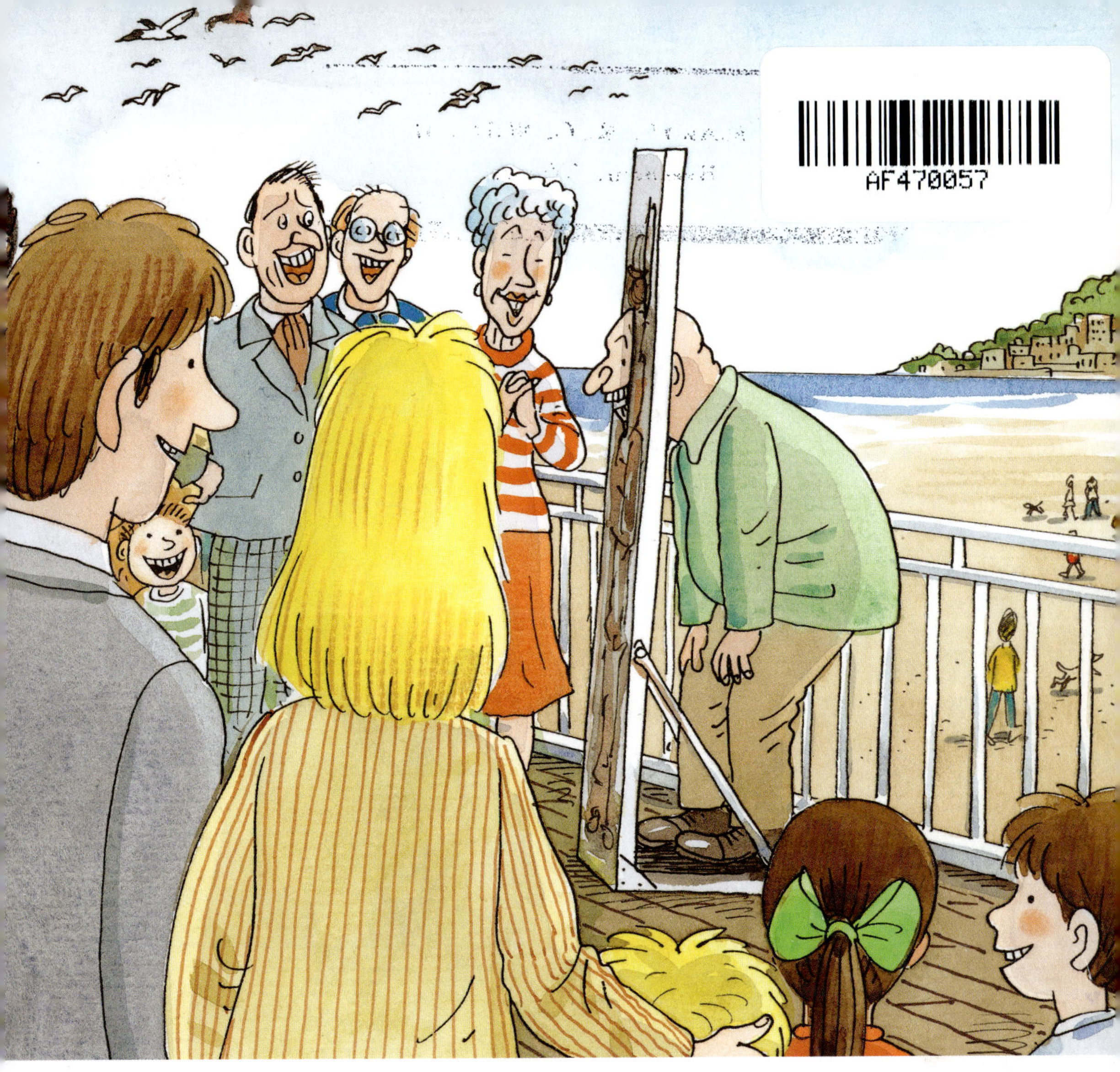

Dad and Mum.

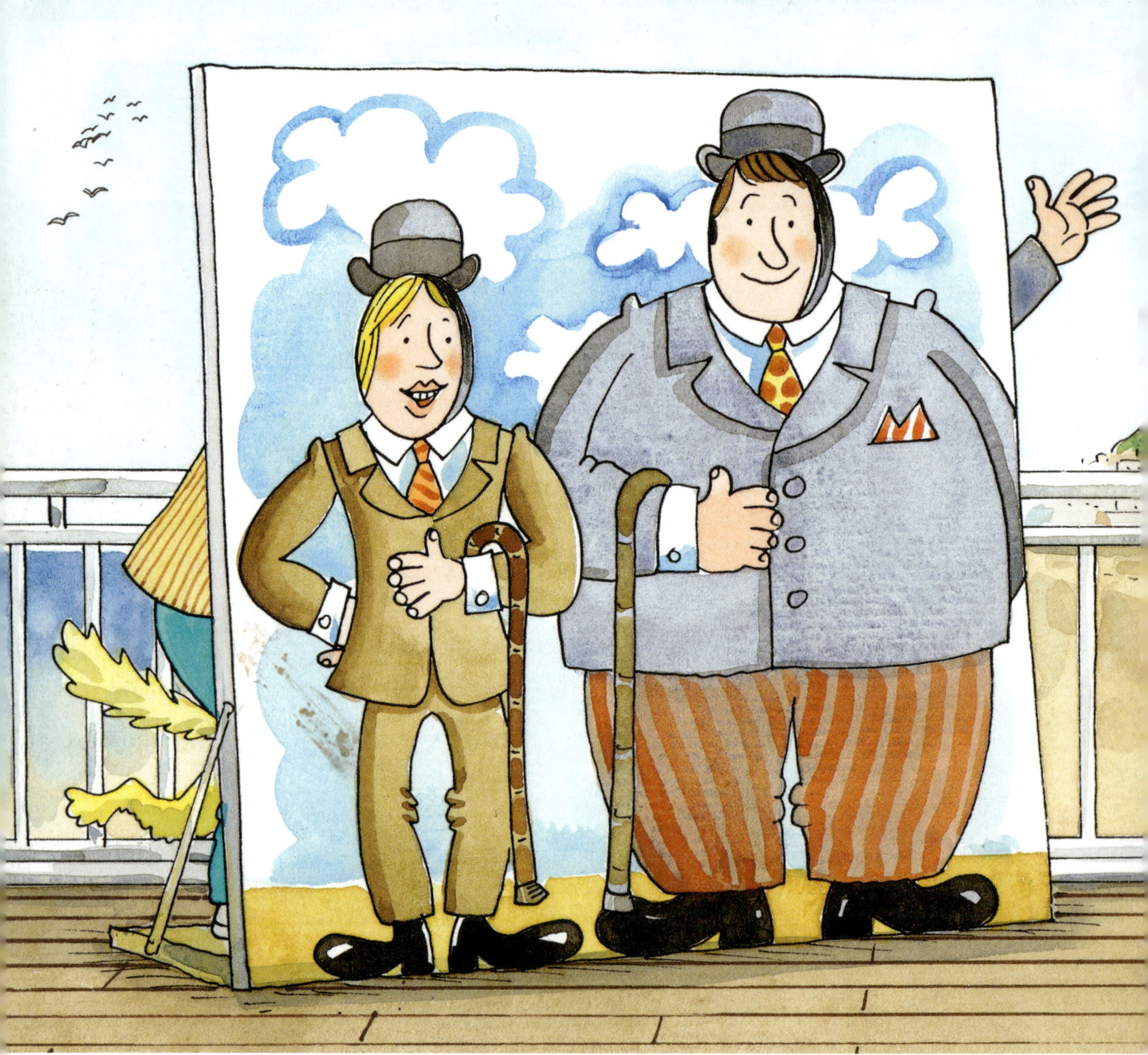

Mum and Dad.

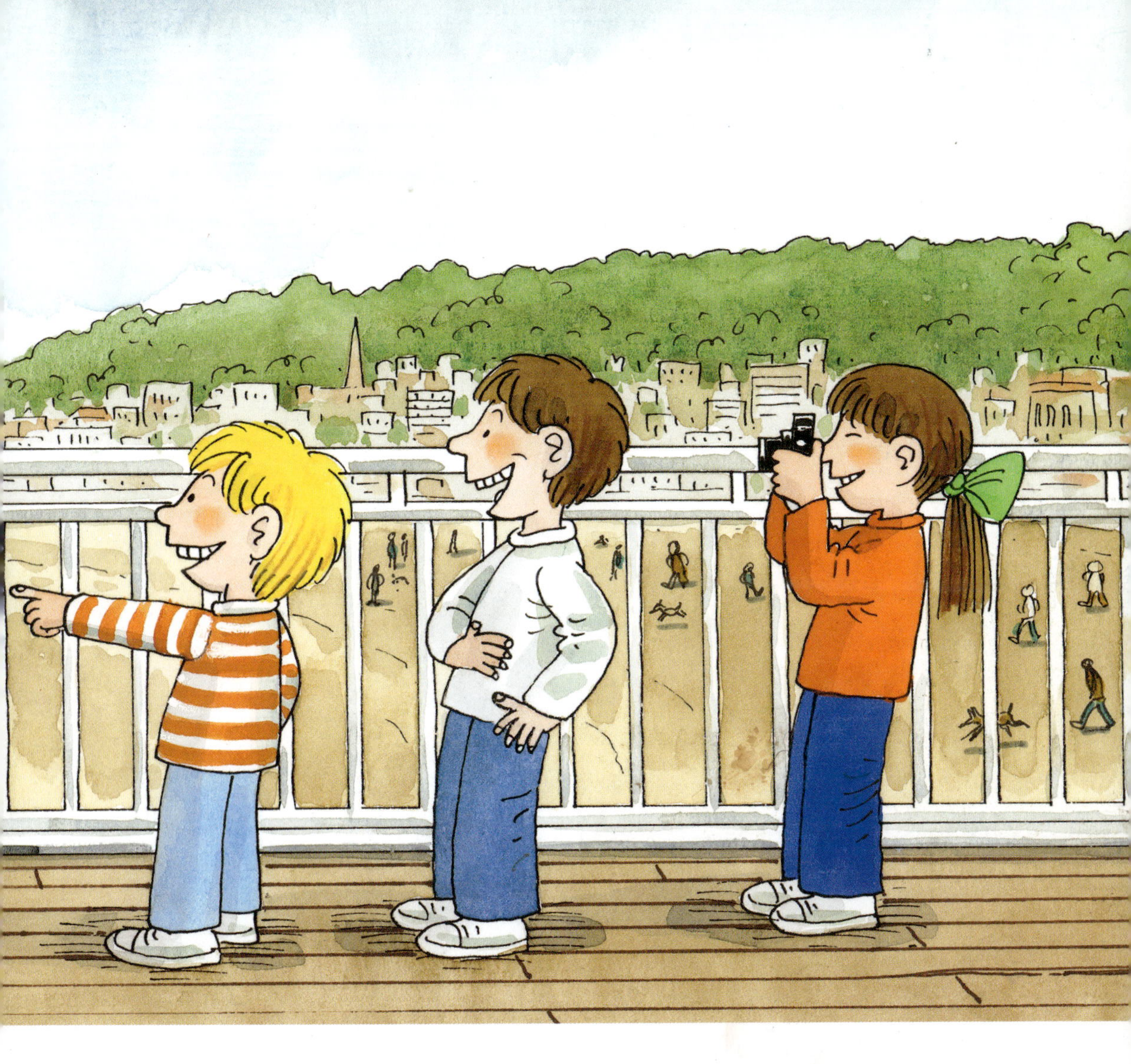

Kipper, Chip and Biff.

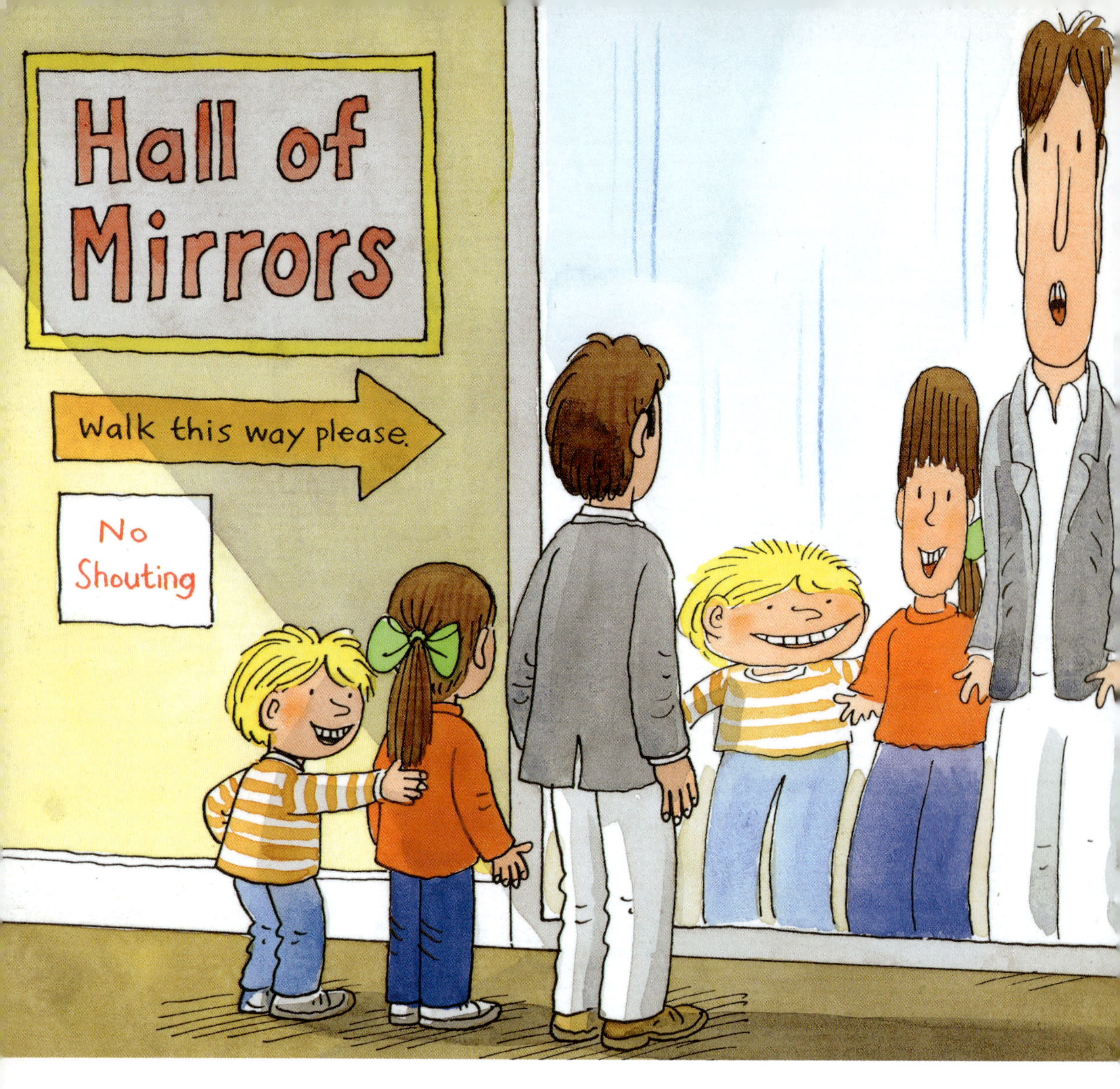

Kipper, Biff and Dad.

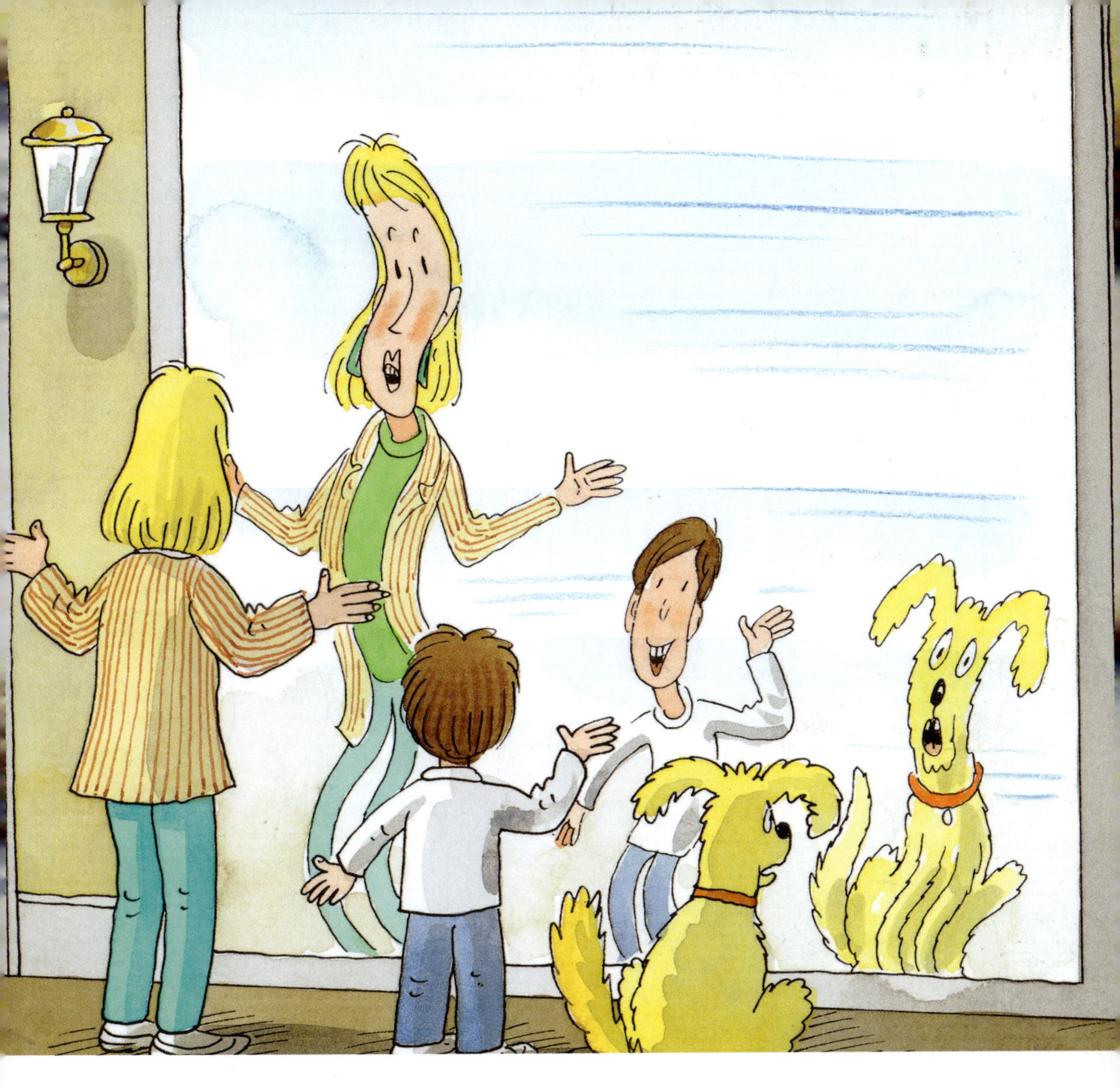

Mum, Chip and Floppy.

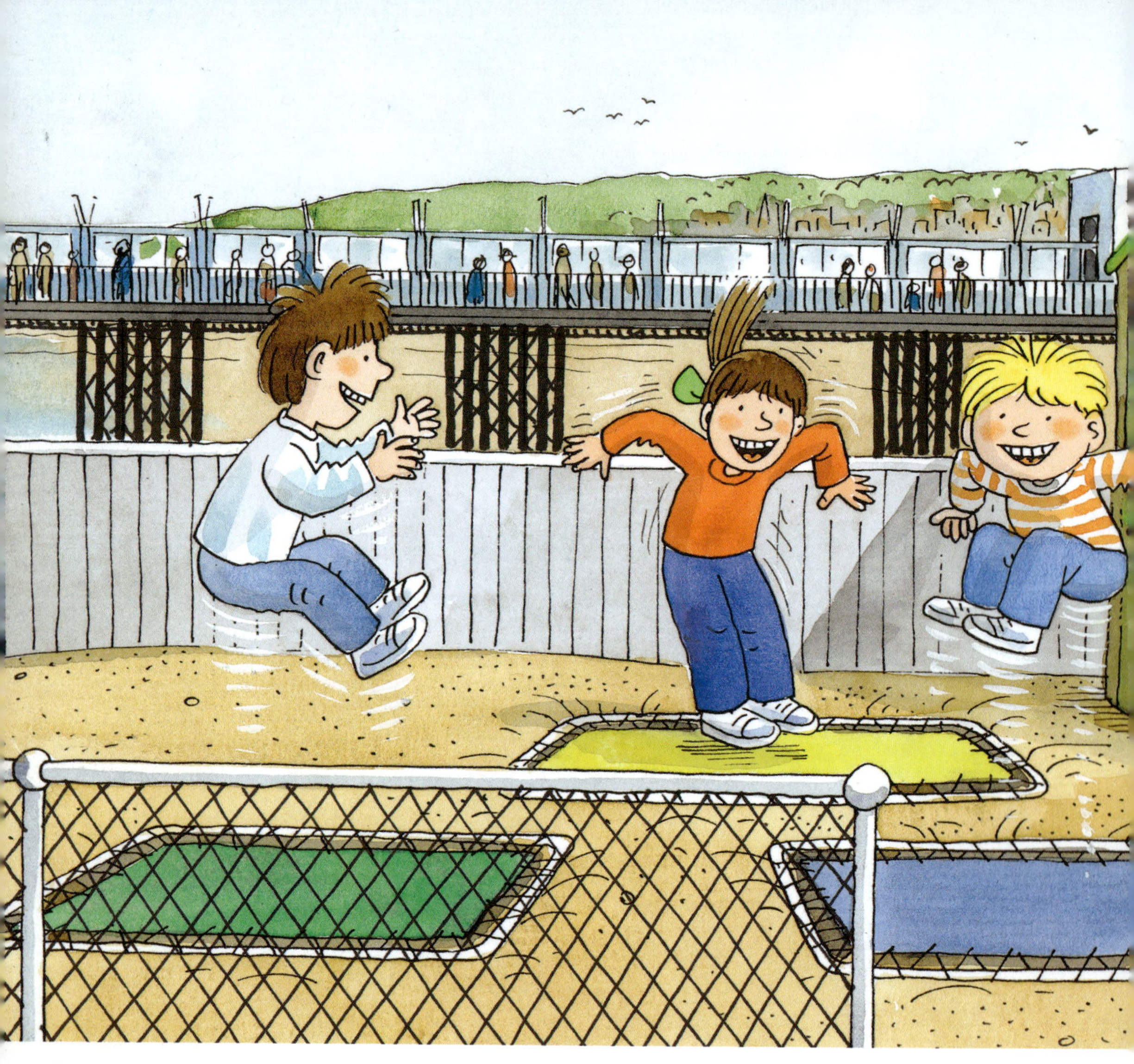

Chip, Biff and Kipper.

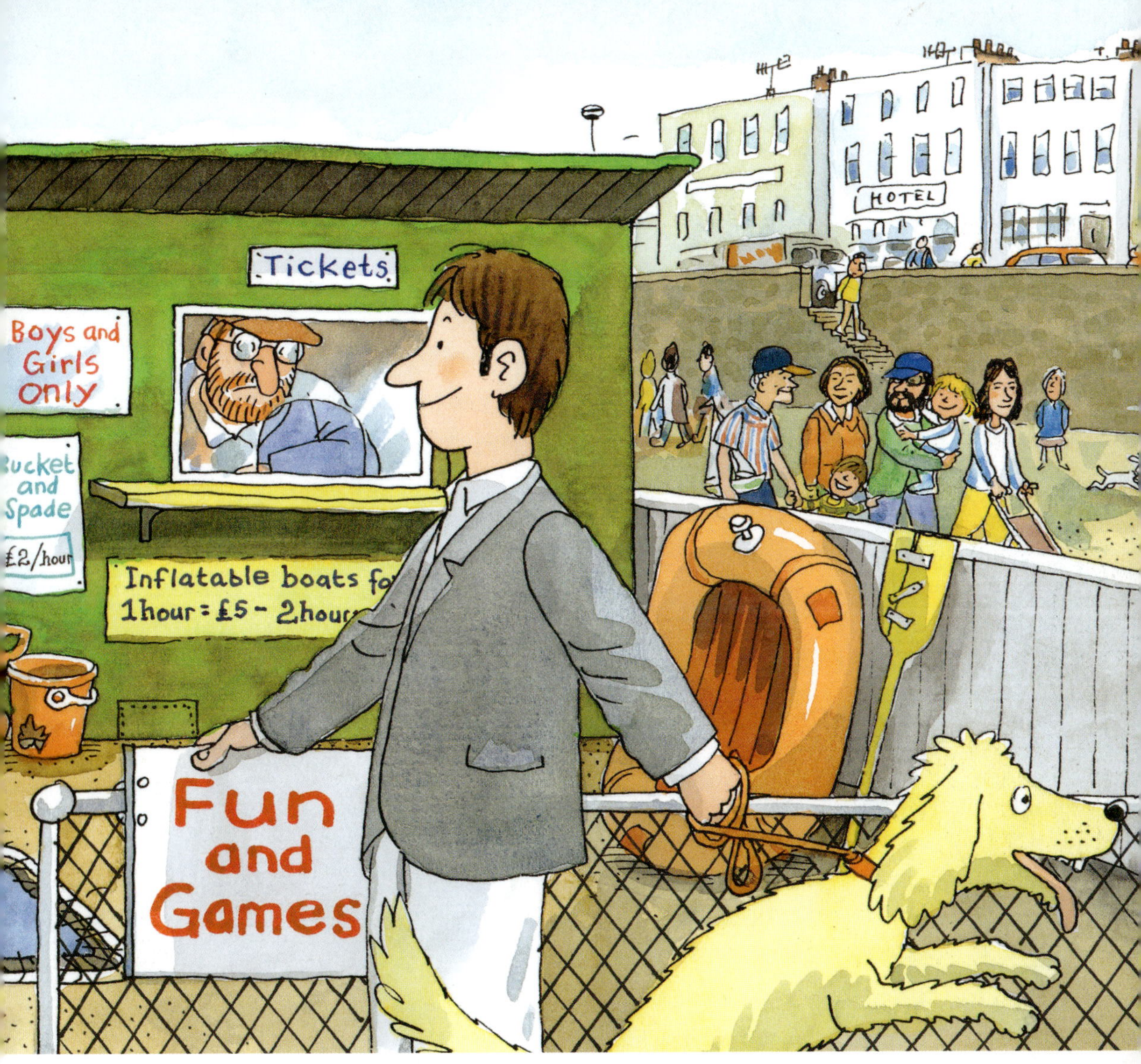

Dad and Floppy.

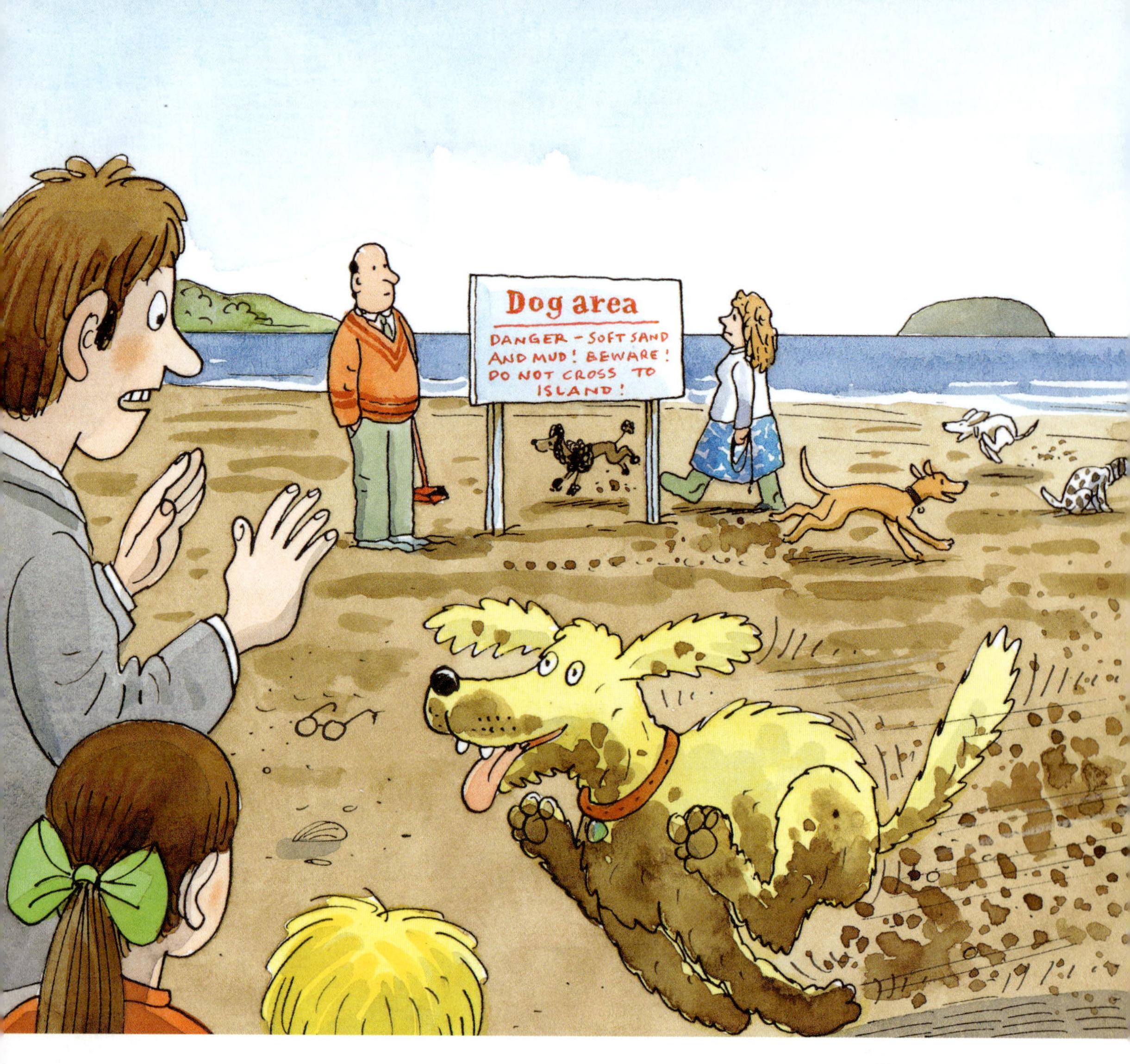
Dog area
DANGER - SOFT SAND
AND MUD! BEWARE!
DO NOT CROSS TO
ISLAND!

Oh Floppy!